BREAKING

THE SHACKLES OF

UNFORGIVENESS

STEPHANIE VANN

BREAKING THE SHACKLES OF UNFORGIVENESS

Stephanie Vann
stephaniebeale43@gmail.com

ISBN 978-1-949826-63-0

Printed in the USA.
All rights reserved

Published by: EAGLES GLOBAL BOOKS | Frisco, Texas
In conjunction with the 2023 Eagles Authors Course
Cover & interior designed by:
Destined To Publish | www.DestinedToPublish.com

DEDICATION

This book is dedicated to my daughters (four girls), who took this journey with me and to those who are struggling with unforgiveness and do not know how to forgive.

Acknowledgments

I want to thank God for never leaving me or forsaking me. Thank You for Your wisdom during the writing of this book. I want to acknowledge my immediate family, my church family, and those with whom I serve in ministry for being an outlet for me through the healing, delivering, and restoration process; they gave me a word of encouragement or a shoulder to cry on, or played a part in my spiritual growth. Without the love and support of my daughters, who encouraged me to tell my story, I would not have been able to help others, who could not forgive for whatever reason.

FOREWORD

This book has a breaker anointing flowing through every word. Stephanie addresses guilt, condemnation, hurt and pain, unforgiveness, and shame. She walks you through her process and the impact on her children. Stephanie also addresses how she overcame and is still working through the process of healing. This book will set so many people free—not just women but also the children who stand beside their moms.

The statement that hit me the most was "Oh, I know that Mommy. That is the real her, from before the marriage." *My God!* This demonstrates how lost we can become and our need to be loved and found by the Father. When I read this book, I just felt deliverance and breakthrough.

Apostle Tamara Nichols
Kingdom Alignment Apostolic Training Center
Newport News, Virginia

CONTENTS

INTRODUCTION

Love is not blind because God is love. However, the wrong love can lead to blindness. Do you ever feel unable to recover from being broken by someone you love or from not loving yourself? As we get older, we start to look over our lives and our visions of what we want them to be. For example, we may want to be married or to have nice homes, children, good jobs, and so on. Notice that I spoke of what we wanted our lives to be. After all, we often forget the most important part: putting God first in everything we do (Matthew 6:33). Not seeking His wisdom, knowledge, or understanding of the choices we make results in dismantled lives. Our Heavenly Father has given us a blueprint for how we should live our lives (Ephesians 1:9–10), an action plan for us to follow straight into God's purpose for our lives.

I will take you on a journey from my brokenness due to unforgiveness to my walking life's victory laps. The journey begins at an earlier stage of my life: when I had not forgiven myself for the sinful life I had lived before graduating from high school. Then the journey moves to how I found victory in God's plan for me. I will share my experience of being broken then my transition to being restored and healed. I will talk about my being blind due to the unforgiveness of loved ones and how both of my marriages ended disastrously, turning into unforgiveness and bitterness.

When betrayal took place, I went through all types of emotions, including taking the blame for the betrayal. The decisions one makes affect them and everyone else that is attached to them. You will see how the decisions made affected my children. Brokenness affects people differently. You will see how long it took me to get to a place of peace versus how long it took my family to be at peace, which shook my family to the core. The process of healing cannot be rushed. Healing is a process that only God can allow. You have to open your heart to receive the healing and to love again.

When devastation happens, we immediately go into panic mode and think according to nature instead of the spirit. If we stay in the carnal mindset, the deliverance and healing process takes longer. The Bible tells us, *"Cast your cares on Him because He careth for you"* (I Peter 5:7 NIV). The restoration process does not happen overnight, and it is not easy. You have to endure a journey. This is a faith walk. We cannot see healing, deliverance, or restoration but we know they are coming by faith. Allow God to do what He does best; see the light at the end of the tunnel through all of the distractions that are in your way. This is where you will find peace, joy, hope, and victory. This journey was not easy for me, but with God, I saw the light. At first, I wanted to keep my story to myself. But I shared it because there were others out there that needed to know they were not alone.

It is time to share my story. My vision is no longer clouded; that which was meant to break me has strengthened me. As I look back over the years, I see the different stages I went through to get where I am now. Here, I will share my journey of being a broken vessel, struggling with forgiveness, having the shattered pieces restored, receiving God's provision, and pushing through the unknown into victory. The journey does not end there. Life is always a journey we must risk taking. Don't be afraid to move from the spot you are at. Along the way, we will run into distractions and setbacks, and we will come to a plain level path where the journey is peaceful. Whichever journey you travel, just know you do not have to take it alone. There is a comforter.

Chapter 1

EARLY YEARS

"Then I acknowledged my sin to you and did not cover up my iniquity. I said, 'I will confess my transgressions to the Lord.' And you forgave the guilt of my sin."
(Psalm 32:5, NIV)

Do you remember when you recognized unforgiveness? I remember wanting attention from boys when I was a teenager. I could not determine if they liked me for me or just wanted one thing from me. Either way, I was receiving attention—the wrong kind of attention. I did not know the word "no." At the age of fifteen, I became pregnant. I did not tell my parents until I was almost three months pregnant. They were so disappointed in me. I was also disappointed in myself. When I informed the person with whom I was pregnant, he said, "Who is the father?" Of course, it was his. At that point, I felt lonely and scared. My parents were upset with me and the father of my baby, denying he was the father. I thought my whole world was over.

I went to school, where my friends looked at me as if I had eggs on my face. Since I was underage, the best thing to do was to get an abortion. I had no say in the matter. No one asked for my opinion. I was too young to make a decision. Back in those days, a child was seen and not heard. To tell you the truth, I wanted to keep my baby. My baby was someone whom I could love and who could love me back, someone besides myself whom I could focus on. When my mother and I pulled up to the Women's Clinic, there were protestors in the parking lot, encouraging women not to kill their babies. I was already scared; seeing them made me feel ashamed too.

Many mixed emotions went through my head. I was a teenager experiencing pregnancy as an adult woman. When I walked into the clinic, there were many people in the waiting room. I think I was the youngest on that day. It was the worst day of my life. We ended the life of an innocent baby, not allowing them to develop fully and live the life they were supposed to live. From that day to the age of twenty-seven years, I lived with unforgiveness for myself. I did not consider the fact that I had been underage and unable to make my own decisions.

In my mind, I kept replaying the words my dad had spoken when he and my mom had found out I was pregnant: "Look at your mother. You are the reason she is crying." *What about me? What about how I felt?* Not once did anyone ask me how I felt. For years, my thought process was that I did not deserve to have any children because I had gotten rid of my baby. I didn't deserve to have a family of my own. I knew it would take a miracle for me to forgive myself. My sister and mother went to church faithfully, but I did not want to set foot inside the church because of my guilt and shame regarding the sin I had lived in previous years. *How could God love me for what I had done?* He couldn't use me, or so I thought.

Once I gave my life to Christ, He forgave me for all my previous sins. I no longer felt ashamed and lonely. I was able to forgive myself for the things I had done. When I gave my life to Christ, I was married to my first husband, and my daughter was four years old. When I had found out I was pregnant with her, the memories had come back. The doctor had told me that I would have a baby. I had broken down and cried; it had been as if I was fifteen years old all over again. After my doctor's appointment, I had walked into my parents' home crying. My sister had been happy for me but had not understood why I was not happy about the good news. She had been unaware of what had happened years before. I had dreaded telling my parents that history was repeating itself. Quickly, I had become that teenage girl again. But their reaction had been the opposite of what I had expected: "Why are you crying? You are grown now."

If we made bad decisions in the past, God can still use us in the future. We have to learn to forgive ourselves and leave our past sins where they belong. The Lord says, *"For I will be merciful toward their iniquities, and I will remember their sins no more"* (Hebrews 8:12, ESV). Our past should not determine our future. To get to where you need to go in life, dig deep and start from the early years. There may be unforgiveness stored deep inside you that needs to be released. After this chapter, I will take you on my journey to breaking free of the shackles of unforgiveness.

"Lord, help us to love ourselves the way You love us, to see ourselves as You see us. The decisions we made in the past do not define who we are today. Thank You for forgiving our sins when we give our lives to You. Show us how to forgive ourselves and others. Father, thank You for looking at our hearts and not our flesh. I pray our relationship with You will increase as we draw closer to You. In Jesus' name, amen!"

REFLECTION:

1. What is the one thing you could not forgive yourself for?

_____

_____

_____

2. Have you forgiven yourself now? Why or why not?

_____

_____

_____

_____

3. What steps did you take in forgiving yourself? What steps might you take if you have not begun the process?

_____

_____

_____

_____

_____

Chapter 2

BROKEN VESSELS

"Yet you, Lord, are our Father. We are the clay, you are the potter; we are all the work of your hand."
(Isaiah 64:8, NIV)

As a little girl, I imagined how my life would be with a family. In a two-person home, both parents work together to provide, protect, and guide the children. That was what I saw while growing up. Again, that was how I was raised—in a two-parent home. So, naturally, I want my home to have both parents. There are bound to be bumps and bruises along the way, and one must be prepared for any issues that arise.

Over time, my marriage came to be based on my obligation to my husband. All I wanted was for my family to be whole and healthy. In life, anything worth having is worth fighting for. Two people become one, representing a family. During my marriage, disaster hit my household more than twice. It was called infidelity. The same behavior showed its ugly face every so often. It was a struggle trying to work through disappointment after disappointment. No matter how hard I tried, the enemy showed up. The third disruption in my household took a toll on the children and me. The only thing I can think of is that whatever you do, it will affect everyone attached to you. This is what we tell the children all the time. I did not know I would have to say the very same thing to my spouse. The disruption in our home was due to infidelity and a woman accusing him of rape. I became numb, showing no emotions. Was this happening to me? I thought, "Father, your word said that you would never leave me nor forsake me; right now, I need you to get through this situation" (Hebrew 13:5, NIV).

I remember feeling disrespected, unwanted, rejected, and so on. Blaming myself was at the top of the list. I kept hearing the words "I love you" from my spouse. Those words meant nothing to me at that point. The same behavior had been happening over and over again: a knife stabbing me in the back and coming out of my chest. That was how I felt about the news I had received. As a wife and mother, I had put my family before myself, and it hurt for someone I truly cared about to stomp on me. I remember the shame I felt every time I walked out of my door.

It seemed as though the whole world knew and was snickering as I walked by. That which had happened in my household was made public on TV and in the newspapers. I received many calls from my family and church family. As the mother of the house, I remained strong for my children, but inside I was crying. At the time, our youngest was eleven or twelve years old. At night, behind closed doors, I would cry into my pillow, asking the Lord to keep me and to help my children and me. I did not want anyone to hear me crying. The children were angry and upset, and felt rejected. They were approached by their friends or their friend's parents, who made comments that left them feeling ashamed and upset.

One thing that I asked God to do was to make sure no one judged the children or me for my husband's actions. At church, everyone knew, but no one asked questions or spoke negatively in front of me. My family and my church family were my biggest supporters during this ordeal. During this time, I was unaware that women at church were scolding my youngest. The women would support me wholeheartedly, but they would call the seed that came from this man "Demon's Child" or treat her differently from the other children. My church family and family were guilty of this. They expected my daughter to make mistakes because she came from a man who was broken, and they imagined his brokenness to be hereditary. Every day, I encouraged her not to make the same mistakes I had made as a child—not accepting myself for who I was and believing the words of others.

It is good to have someone you trust by your side through the process of trying to get your life back on track. We had mornings when I made her stand in front of the mirror and repeat affirmations after me so that she would build her confidence. I did not want her to feel like her life was already written before it had even started. To her, I might have seemed too harsh, but from my perspective, I was refusing to let the devil work any harder than he already had. I kept saying, "Lord, you would never leave me nor forsake me." (Hebrews 13:5 NKJV) I lived by this scripture every day.

My youngest daughter was our child. My husband and I had a combined family. In our household, there were no stepchildren or half-siblings. We leaned on each other to get through the process. When the first incident happened, of course, I was devastated. I was ready to leave, but during my prayer, the Holy Spirit told me "No. You stay." People thought I was crazy for staying, but I was following the voice of the Holy Spirit. I was also thinking of the vows I had taken on my wedding day:

for better or for worse, in sickness and in health, until death do us part. I remember asking myself, "Why am I being made an example of before the world?" As I said, the story was on TV and in the newspaper. Even though my family and church family supported me, I felt alone. One late night, a group of young people knocked on the door and yanked the screen door open. That was a scary moment for us. On another day, I came home and there was a note on the door asking me, "Do you know who you married, and you have your daughter in that house? How could you stay in that house with him and your child?" I felt like a bad parent.

I love my family. No family is perfect. If we were perfect, we wouldn't need God. We live in a world where people just don't care what they say or do to others and what effects their actions have on others. My husband was not a bad person. He taught the girls how to change a flat tire so that when the time came for them to drive, they would know what to do if no one else was around. In the trunk, he would have jumper cables, and he made sure there was a spare tire and a jack in every car. He also taught the girls how to cut grass. Whenever someone needed anything, he went out of his way to provide it if he could. We made sure we were all together for dinner on most nights, and we would talk about our day. This gave the girls space to share. Even if some things were held back, we allowed them to share. Quality time was big for him as well: riding bikes to get ice cream, taking them camping in the backyard, and cooking with our youngest after the older girls left for college. He made sure they had some experience and would not depend on a man to do the basics. There were some good times during our marriage. Our household was a Christian home. I would not have had it any other way.

When things go wrong in life, some people tend to run away from God instead of running to Him for protection, peace, joy, healing, and deliverance. Mental health expert Judith Herman [1] says, "Healing from trauma involves making meaning of the trauma event. This event often confuses people because it does not make sense. Trauma differs from expectations." I understand her reasoning. I said at the beginning of this chapter that to me, a family was made up of a husband, a wife, and children because that was how I was raised. That was my expectation of marriage. So when the trauma happened, I was confused.

Yes, I know marriage is not perfect. You have to work at it every day. I had not expected the trauma that my family experienced. Yet, through all of the hurt and pain that we experienced as a family, I was there to support my husband. People thought I was crazy to support him after what he had put us through: "Why would you support someone after the things he chose to do?" Just because something awful happened, it does not mean that the love is gone. I never used the situation against him. I forgave him, but I did not forget. Over the years, there was a second time and then a third one. I asked God again, "Lord, what now? Should I still stay? This is painful. Enough is enough."

God released me. The third time was a doozy. During the whole ordeal, I had not spoken negatively about him. Whenever the children spoke negatively, I tried to turn it around. Of course, they did not understand why I would do that after everything we had been through and were continuing to go through. It felt like my whole world had just stopped. Out of all the children, my youngest daughter took it the hardest. She had lost her example of a male who was supposed to protect her. She put a wall up. I was there for comfort and direction, letting her know that her feelings were valid, but we were meant to forgive. The way she looked at me, it was as if I was speaking a strange language.

When I think about it, I realize I had put a wall up too. I didn't allow people to get close to me and thought everyone had a hidden agenda. I leaned on my Heavenly Father even more, asking Him to keep us, comfort us, and protect us. He did just that. There began to be some sleepless nights and some crying here and there. During this time, receiving phone calls from my husband did not make it any better. I asked him "Why? Why?" He responded that he didn't know. Later, he explained that I had always been in church, and he had felt left behind. The crazy part of all this was that he had been in church too. He had also owned a business that had kept him busy. I thank God that the opportunity came for me to take training modules in dance. A church member introduced me to the training institute. To me, it was the best thing ever. There was true love from everyone. It did not matter if they knew you or not. The Eagles Network (TEN) changed my life. It opened my eyes not only to ministering in movement but also to my relationship with God.

When I started TEN, the first incident had already happened. We were piecing our broken family back together. It was a struggle, but we pressed through. After my first Summit in Dallas, Texas, I came home and told my family that from that day forward, our lives would never be the same. We had to be prepared. I knew then that I had been elevated to another level in Him. I was no longer the same person spiritually. That was why my husband felt left behind. I grew spiritually and tried to take him where he was not willing to go just yet. I had become part of a worldwide family. On those bad days, I had someone who was always there to encourage me and speak a word. They had no idea what I was going through or how much I needed it.

I still felt alone physically because no one knew what was going on and I dared not say anything, or so I thought. I did not want to be judged. Only those who were very close to me knew what was happening. It was a time when I felt unloved by a person I had thought would protect me. I had put my trust and faith in a person, not God. The Bible tells us, *"It is better to trust in the Lord than to put confidence in man"* (Psalm 118:8, KJV). That was my first mistake: not trusting God. That was when I realized I had a long road of healing and deliverance ahead of me.

"Heavenly Father, I pray for families that are going through rough times. Strengthen their households right now at the sound of my voice. They are complete units. Satan, count yourself noticed. I command you to take your hands off the family unit. You have no dominion or power over the family unit. Father, I pray they keep You first in their lives. We know we are not perfect, but we know all things are possible through You. I pray they will put their trust in You in everything they put their hands to. Thank You for putting their vessel back together again with love. In Jesus' name, amen!"

REFLECTION:

1. What are some life experiences that have left you broken?

_____

_____

_____

_____

2. How did they make you feel?

_____

_____

_____

_____

3. What did God show you about yourself in those moments?

_____

_____

_____

_____

Chapter 3

STRUGGLE WITH FORGIVENESS

"Bear with each other and forgive one another
if any of you has a grievance against someone.
Forgive as the Lord forgave you."
(Colossians 3:13, NIV)

This was how I felt over the years: hurt, rejected, disrespected, deceived, and unloved. The spirit of unforgiveness brought on the spirit of bitterness. As a believer, I know that God instructs us to forgive and the forgiveness is for us, not for the person who wronged us (Colossians 3:13). But my flesh says I have been rejected, I have been deceived, I have been disrespected, and I have been hurt.

When I was married to my first husband, he was stationed on the West Coast for a few years. My daughter and I stayed on the East Coast since he was not going to be there for more than three years. Our relationship suffered due to the distance between us. I did not agree to the long-distance relationship. I had my doubts about our marriage's survival. I was right, it did not last the first year after he left due to his infidelity and unwillingness to work it out. This was a doozy. I became bitter and unforgiveness crept in—not only of him but also of myself. I began asking myself that familiar question: "What did I do wrong?" This is the first question you ask yourself when things don't work out. A lot of the time, though, it is not your fault. The other person has a choice and makes a decision that may or may not affect you.

I recall that years later, after our divorce, I made a comment to my ex-husband that was harsh. Out of hurt, bitterness, and unforgiveness, I said, "The best part of our marriage was having our daughter and talking to your brother about Christ because in return, he received salvation." *Ouch!* From the look on his face, I could see I had hurt his feelings. I felt so bad about what I had said, but I was still hurting. I wanted him to feel my pain. During our unforgiveness, we need to be mindful of others' feelings even if they are the people who hurt us.

After my divorce, six years later, I married my high school sweetheart. We had gone our separate ways after graduating high school but had kept in touch. We had both married other people. Then we had eventually ended up together again and had combined our families. Like my first marriage, my second marriage struggled due to infidelity. We tried to work through it, but it was difficult as the same thing kept happening. I felt that my second husband took advantage of my forgiving him after each occurrence.

At that point, I felt there were no good men in the world. That was why I asked God again, "Did I do anything wrong? What should I have done differently?" I started to blame myself for my relationships going in a direction opposite of what I would have liked. That was the problem: "what I would have liked." I had to repent and ask for forgiveness for not consulting God before deciding to marry either man. In my first marriage, I was not saved. I didn't know better. We were young when we got married and had no idea what to do in a marriage. In the second marriage, I was saved and filled with the Holy Spirit and still did not consult God. This time, I knew better. You know the saying "You do better when you know better"? My flesh tells me, "I am grown and I can make my own decisions." My predicament was the result of that: In both marriages, I saw the red flags and still went ahead.

As a result of both marriages, my daughters suffered. My oldest daughter asked me, "Am I the reason why my daddy is no longer here?" Try explaining to a four-year-old why her father left. One thing I did not do was talk negatively about him. Anything she needed to know; I referred her back to him. My heart was broken whenever he promised he would come then did not show up, disappointing her. The road to forgiveness would take some time—not for me but for my daughter. I blamed myself for hurting her. I had to forgive myself for not consulting God first for me and for our children.

Not too long ago, my children told me they had unforgiveness towards me. I knew that what had happened had affected them, but they're not forgiving me for what was going on in the house made me feel like a failure immediately. I was trying to keep my family together. So many marriages ended due to cheating, and I did not want to be part of the statistics. I guess it had all become too much for me to handle. My oldest daughter left home to stay with my parents. This was after the first cheating episode had occurred and the young lady had accused him of rape. His aggressive discipline was sometimes overbearing and did not help the situation. My first husband wanted to come and get my oldest daughter. The only reason he did not come was that my parents allowed her to stay with them until she graduated from high school. When my daughter left to stay with my parents, I felt crushed. I did not want her to think that I did not love her or had chosen my husband over her. I was still trying to fix the family. My daughters' opinion was that I had chosen the behavior of my husband over the safety and well-being of my children. I had to sit and listen to everything they expressed to me whether I wanted to hear it or not. I was choosing my family, but they did not see it that way.

As parents, we have to apologize for the part we play in hurting our children. We are not perfect. Some of our decisions are not the right ones at a given time. There is no time limit on forgiving a person. I remained strong in front of our daughters even though my face said something different. My youngest daughter was nearly a teenager. She was at an easily influenced age, and there was no male figure in the home and no example of how a male should treat her, no man to protect and guide her. Yes, I was there, but God's order had been stripped from our home. I had to be an example of a strong Christian woman before her and had to show how to be led by God in every area of my life, even when it hurt. Was I a robot? No. I was just striving to be the best version of myself in a tough situation.

Members of our extended family—his side of the family and mine—were struggling with unforgiveness as well. My family supported me in my decision but preferred him not to be around, and he knew that. I was stuck in the middle.

This was not a great place to be—I would listen to what they had to say about what I needed to do and then what he had to say about how my family was treating him. They only wanted the best for me. No parent wants to see their child hurt. It was exhausting. When we had family functions, my husband still attended them though he knew how everyone felt about him. He came to support me, not them. After I repented and God forgave me, I asked the Father to help me forgive my spouse for cheating on me and not choosing his family first.

After the previous incidents, I had forgiven him and had not looked back, but this one was different. I struggled for years to forgive him. Even after he apologized for hurting me. My mouth said, "Yes, I forgive him," and I thought I had. However, when he called to speak with our daughter and me, my anger rose again, especially when he wanted to talk about our relationship. "What relationship? There is no relationship!" I would reply. Yes, I was speaking out of hurt and operating out of flesh.

One thing that I did not hold back from expressing was how I had felt when the incident first happened and how I felt at that moment. During one of his phone calls, he told me I cared nothing about him and that if I was a Christian, I would not break up the family. At that point, I was boiling. What gave him the right to say I was not a Christian woman when I refused to take him back? The children were over eighteen years old. They were no longer children. That was an example of not allowing others to speak in one's ear about things that were not true. During our marriage, I had held my tongue to keep peace in the house. We have to choose our battles. I am so glad God put people in my life to support and guide me through the process. I drew closer to God and focused more on the purpose God had for me in the Kingdom. According to Los Angeles Christian Counseling [2], there are eight steps to true forgiveness:

1. Acknowledge the pain.
2. Think through things.
3. Imagine being on the other side.
4. Remember God's forgiveness.
5. Reflect on our Biblical command.
6. Let go of the hurt.
7. Continue to forgive.
8. Pray for the person who hurt you.

I acknowledged the pain; it hurt. As I had previously forgiven, the forgiveness did not happen this time around. In prayer, I begged the Father to take away the pain. I had to decide whether to stay or to leave. I knew I could not make a decision based on my emotions. My mind and heart had to be clear. I spent time with God, and we went back and forth; He spoke, and I spoke. He instructed me to forgive.

My response was to wonder how I could forgive when I was in so much pain. That was when I had to think through what had happened. I realized that while we were hurting, my husband was hurting too. He was separated from his family and alone. He had no one to tell how his day was going. He missed out on seeing the girls getting older and with their own families. He missed high school graduation, weddings, and life experiences with the girls. In life, you make so many wrong choices throughout the day, not knowing which one will destroy you. Whatever you do affects you and everyone attached to you.

God says, *"For if you forgive other people when they sin against you, your heavenly Father will also forgive you"* (Matthew 6:14 NIV). Let's think about that for a minute. That one scripture says a lot. God commands us to forgive. When we sin against Him, He forgives us over and over and over. So when someone does something against us, we should forgive them. We sin easily when we do not forgive the other person. Take a moment and let that settle. When we take long to forgive others, it takes God the same amount of time to forgive us. That is why forgiveness is for you, not for the other person. The longer you walk around with unforgiveness in your heart, the longer the hurt will be in your heart.

Asking God to take away your pain every day does nothing. Forgiveness is an action word. Speaking it with your mouth does nothing. I had to stop rehearsing the betrayal in my head and getting even more upset. It was making it last longer. I still answered my husband's calls, but I only did so when I wanted to, not out of obligation. When I realized I did not have to answer every time he called, the pain eased. I needed time and space to heal without distractions from him. At first, he could not understand why I needed time and space. Eventually, he gave me the time and space to clear my head and receive the healing I needed. But he told me, "You never loved me." *Really!*

The Father had to work on me. I was a mess emotionally, and no one knew. You know how we wear masks, hiding what is affecting us and claiming everything is ok with smiles on our faces. I had to literally cast everything onto the Father's shoulders and leave it there. While in prayer, asking God to get me through the ordeal, I included my husband in the prayer. It was a genuine prayer, not a prayer of hurt. No matter what had transpired between us, he still needed prayer. At times, during his telephone calls, we prayed together over the children, our health, and whatever else was going on. This was a sign that forgiveness was starting and it was a process. No one can tell you how long forgiveness will take, but it has to take place to free you from the bondage of unforgiveness.

"Heavenly Father, I pray for others who are not able to forgive. Forgiveness is for them and not for the people who hurt them. Restore their peace and joy. Give them the strength to endure the hurt so that they may use the hurt to enter into your presence and so that they may know that it is you who restores. It is you who gives strength. In your presence, every weight is removed from their shoulders, making their burdens lighter to carry. Father, I thank you for the intimate relationship they will experience with you. They will receive your love, kindness, grace, and mercy. Father, I ask you to give them wisdom that surpasses all understanding. Let them experience how much you love them and show them how to forgive those who hurt them. They will walk in freedom with nothing limiting them from walking into their next. In Jesus' name, amen"

REFLECTIONS:

1. Who is a person you have not forgiven yet? Why?

_____

_____

_____

_____

_____

2. Have you acknowledged the wrong they have done to you? Why or why not?

_____

_____

_____

_____

_____

_____

_____

_____

3. Have you truly given it over to God? Why or why not?

_____

_____

_____

_____

_____

_____

_____

4. Has forgiveness taken place? How do you know?

_____

_____

_____

_____

_____

_____

_____

_____

Chapter 4

RESTORING SHATTERED PIECES

How long will this feeling last? That was the question I asked myself time and time again. Everyone has an opinion. People give you advice based on their feelings or emotions. There are therapists out there who have the credentials to help you. Some people do not like to see a therapist—it's the idea of telling a perfect stranger all of their business. You also have your pastor or someone older who can give you wise counsel. There are so many layers of emotions to look beneath. As for me, I went to the very person I could rely on: God. He knew how I was feeling and what I was going through. I could not wear a mask in His presence like I could with others. I was an emotional wreck, and no one knew it but God. While I was in the presence of God, He reminded me of His word: *"Come to me, all you who are weary and burdened, and I will give you rest"* (Matthew 11:28, NIV). We cannot carry every load we encounter alone. We have to release it to move forward. God wants us to come to him. He will not beg us or force us to. We have a choice. He loves and cares for us. We will find rest in Him. When the Spirit speaks, listen and move.

There were times when I questioned what the Spirit was saying to me, and I missed the mark. Isn't that what the Holy Spirit is for? He is our Comforter if we just listen the first time. As flesh, we want to be in control of our own lives. We make decisions based on emotions. Our emotions and pride will lead us in the wrong direction. According to *Merriam Webster* [3], pride is "the quality or state of being proud: such as reasonable self-esteem: confidence, and satisfaction in oneself."

Pride is hard to break because we think we do not need anyone and can do everything ourselves. We believe that only we know what is best for us. But we should set down the pride and accept help. God places others in our lives to be a blessing to us. It is ok to accept blessings. This was hard for me—even now, it still is hard at times. I do not want to be a burden to others. They have their own lives. But how can I make decisions for someone else and not allow them the opportunity to be a blessing to me?

There were times when people would walk up to me and say some encouraging words right when I needed to hear them. Do not disregard such encouraging words. God placed them in these people's hearts so that they would release them to you. In addition to the encouraging words, God made it so that these people would help you with what you needed. We miss out when we do not listen to God. We cannot say we trust Him and then not do what He says. There have been times when God has told me to go to a certain person because they have what I need. It has been hard to approach that person and ask for help. There it is again: *pride*. When are we going to stop thinking we can go through life without anyone's help? When we don't accept help, we are also saying we won't take help from God. Allow God to lead you to the people from whom you can receive the resources you need without their asking or expecting something in return.

Can I tell you something? The person you are going to was already told to bless you. They are just waiting for you to approach them. Comfort is not the only thing I have experienced in the presence of God. I have also experienced God's love and grace. Experiencing love does not happen overnight. It is a process.

Yes, we know God loves us, but we have to receive His love. We are worthy of receiving love from the Father. I know it is hard to think that someone loves you that much, but He does. He loves you so much that He gave His only son for you. While growing up, I sometimes felt I was not loved. But my family loved me. I received a revelation: "You think no one loves you because you do not love yourself." You see how your mind can tell you, "No one loves me"?

As I got older, I wondered what true love felt and looked like. People try to find true love in others. But people cannot give other people the level of love they receive from God. So, when my marriage was in danger of falling apart due to infidelity, I was devastated. I had relied on my spouse to make me complete. Better yet, I had thought both of us would be complete because we had each other. I had put my trust in the wrong person. God cared for me so much that He wanted me to be made whole. What did that look like? Being made whole was being healthy in mind, body, and soul: completely restored. I may not be completely there. Who is? But I am not where I was over six years ago.

The phone calls from my husband have decreased dramatically. Without the distractions from the phone calls, I am more relaxed and at peace. There has to be a change in you when the shattered pieces of your heart are being put back together. Your mind goes from cloudy to clear. I had to put some self-care in place for myself. On my bathroom mirror, there are affirmation statements that I speak to myself before leaving the house. There are also affirmations for my daughter.

I remember my daughter once thought she was ugly. So every morning, she had to recite the affirmations. We always tell her that she is beautiful and smart and she can do anything she puts her mind to. Now, when people tell her she is not attractive, she tells them, "That is your opinion. I am beautiful and I know who I am." Affirmations work. They give you a sense of empowerment and command your day.

Some of the affirmations we had on our mirrors follow:

1. I am loved.
2. I am beautiful.
3. I am enough.
4. I am highly favored.
5. I am the head and not the tail.
6. I am strong.
7. I am a child of the Most High.
8. I am rich and not poor.

9. I am smart.

The best part of knowing that the pieces are being put back together is loving who I am without someone telling me who I am. None of this would be possible if I had continued to hold unforgiveness in my heart and thought I was not enough.

"Father, I pray for those who are broken and seeking ways to put their shattered pieces back together. The pieces cannot be put together without You. I pray that they come into Your presence with open hearts and minds to receive instructions from You as well as mercy, grace, and love. Agape love doesn't require explanations of why You love them so much. I speak life into their situations. There is hope in You, Lord. I pray their faith will increase as they trust You more regarding how their lives will turn around for the better. Thank You for the mindset that will shift during this period of shattered pieces' being put back together. The pieces will be stronger than ever and will be able to stand during difficult times. This will work if they deny themselves, eliminating pride. Pride has no room where the Holy Spirit lives. In Jesus' name, amen."

REFLECTIONS:

1. Have you started to put the shattered pieces together? Why or why not?

_____

_____

_____

2. What steps did you take in order to put the pieces back together? What steps will you take?

_____

_____

_____

3. What affirmation statements, if any, helped you through the process? If you haven't used any, what affirmation statements might you adopt?

_____

_____

_____

_____

Chapter 5

GOD'S PROVISION

"But seek first his kingdom and his righteousness,
and all these things will be given to you as well."
(Matthew 6:33, NIV)

Citing Matthew 6:33 has become very important to me through this process of moving forward no matter what my past looks like. My thought process was that I should not expect anything from anyone. That way, I couldn't get hurt emotionally or spiritually. I know that is not the way to be. My mouth was saying, "Lord, I will seek you first," but my mind wanted to be in control and have me do everything for myself.

We all need someone we can rely on and talk to, someone to encourage us and positively push us. To see a change in your life, you have to seek the Father with your whole heart and surrender to Him. He wants your undivided attention. You cannot walk this earth with walls built around you, not allowing others to speak into your life or lend a helping hand. It took a while for me to realize that when I did not allow others to bless me, I was not allowing God to bless me through them. I am enough, and I deserve everything God has for me. People are placed in my life for a reason and a season, with pure intentions and led by God. Once I realized that there was a wall around me, preventing me from receiving fully from God, I had to repent and surrender. Yes, you have to relinquish control. It is a scary thing not knowing what lies ahead. Giving up control puts you in a vulnerable state.

Doors started to open. I got a promotion at work. When my manager retired, I was automatically promoted to her position. I had received no formal training from my employer. But my manager taught me what she knew over fifteen years. So, when she was no longer there, I knew how to function as a manager. It was hands-on training. Another one of God's provisions was protection from an accident that should have killed my family and I. One night in the summer, I was driving home from my sister's house with my aunt and daughter. The interstate had no lights, and I drove up on a tree that had fallen across two lanes. I noticed the tree at the last minute when it was too late to switch lanes. I saw my life flashing before me. I thought the car would hit the tree and flip over. Instead, I drove through the tree. The tree was old and weak. *Praise the lord!* Thank You, Father, for Your protection and grace. The car took us all the way home without any hesitation. We had no scratches, but our hearts were beating out of our chests. God was so good.

Another accident involved my daughter. She called me to let me know she had gotten into an accident. When I got to the scene, the front of her car was smashed into her steering wheel. She was standing on the side of the road: She had no scratches, nothing was broken, and she was walking and talking. *Glory!* God makes provisions for us. When you go back and think about everything you have gone through in life, you will notice the provisions God made for you. I prefer to be in the background, not out front being seen. I stayed in the background for years until 2013. Now, I sometimes think back and realize how far I have come with the provision of God. I cannot allow walls to block me from receiving the promises and blessings of God.

As a young girl, I had very low self-esteem: "I am not pretty enough. I am too dark; my nose is too big. No one likes me. No one wants me." Does this sound familiar? You know the saying "An idle mind is the devil's playground." This is so true, especially when you are young and do not know what is going on. You start to believe what you have spoken into your life or what others have spoken into your life. You have to speak life into yourself when no one else is around. Yes, it is difficult to encourage yourself when you are going through difficult times. God did not tell you that you were not pretty enough, you couldn't do anything right, and you were not enough. That was the voice of the enemy speaking death into your life.

Every obstacle you encounter can be used to strengthen and build you. It may be easy to sit there and rehash your previous steps, but it is time to get up and put your best foot forward. You may not know every step you have to make. You may think you are not the right person to do what is necessary. This is where God comes in with a provision for your life.

I won a Woman of the Year award from ACHI Magazine (www. achimagazine.com 2022). I had been nominated for three categories: Woman of Inspiration, Difference Maker, and Woman of the Year. ACHI Magazine honors the contributions of extraordinary women working in various fields in their local area. When I was nominated for the three categories, I was honored and appreciative that others saw the associated qualities in me. You know we are our worst critics, right? I am still in awe that I was named Woman of the Year. If someone had told me beforehand that it would happen, I would not have believed them. I also received the Encouragement of the Year award from the Transformation Worship Ministry. I had always prayed that God would allow me to love others as He loved. One way to love is to encourage others. The encouragement you give others will encourage you in turn. For years, the Holy Spirit showed me an apostolic training center, but I did not think I was qualified or gifted enough to pioneer a training center. Oasis Apostolic Training Center started in May 2022.

I am present to help with whatever someone else needs. When the Holy Spirit shows you something, He has made provision for it. He does not want you to do it alone. You will receive resources. People will be put into place to help you with the vision. These are small blessings but major milestones in this season. When I helped others, I was not seeking recognition. When you are in prayer, asking the Lord to enlarge your territory and to use you when He needs you, be prepared.

I was so busy being an instrument for God, I was not thinking about the impact it would have on others. All resources, directions, and doors are open to you. If by chance, a door is not open to you, do not get discouraged and turn back. That particular door is not meant for you. Surrender your will today and receive the will of the Father and His provision for your life.

I recall a conversation I had with my oldest daughter about leaving her job and starting her own business. She told me it had all begun before her marriage. The example of entrepreneurship she had seen while growing up had not been positive—its purpose had not been to obtain wealth but to get further and further into debt, which had created an unhealthy environment for a marriage. She mentioned how she saw me working hard to make sure our home had what we needed. She had observed that my husband had his own business, but we still struggled.

This had created fear and self-doubt inside her, which had prevented her from doing what God had been calling her to do. It had also created monetary trust issues between her and her husband based on what she had seen growing up and not on what she had experienced firsthand in her marriage. After running her business part-time while working full-time for almost two years, she heard the Holy Spirit say that she was to leave her job if she truly trusted Him. Although she was scared, my walk with Christ and its development over the years inspired her belief that God would open doors and provide the resources she needed to move forward in serving her community. I will never forget her telling me how she had seen my life change for the better: If He had done it for me, then He could most certainly do it for her.

Trusting God, she was obedient and surrendered. As a result, the Lord has provided her with coaches, mentors, and colleagues to help her thrive in her business full-time. She started a tax and accounting firm that helped her to overcome in the area in her life in which she needed God the most, and she is also helping others break generational curses. Today, her husband leads their family and raises their two children while working from home. She has helped others break generational financial curses for almost two years. Thanks to God's provision, many doors have opened for her and her husband financially.

"Lord, I speak into the lives of those who think they are not enough because of what people might have spoken to them or the thoughts that their minds whispered to them. They are enough, and they are made in Your image; they are good. Casting down all strongholds and imaginations that are not positive, cover them in Your blood and wash those negative thoughts from their memories so they can move forward in You. Your promises are true and never come back to You void. They are not their past mistakes or hurts. They are loved. I speak life, not death. Father, I speak to their hardened hearts. Chip away at the walls around their hearts so they can receive Your love and provision. I pray for the intimacy they will have when they come into Your presence. Open the right doors for them, and do not allow the wrong doors to open. Lord, give them discernment in every decision they make so that they may surrender their wills and receive Your will in their lives. In Jesus' name, amen!"

REFLECTIONS:

1. What are some of the negative thoughts you have had about yourself?

_____

_____

_____

_____

_____

_____

2. What effect did the negative thoughts have on you?

_____

_____

_____

_____

_____

_____

3. As you think back over your life, what have some of God's provisions for you been?

_____

_____

_____

_____

_____

4. Have you surrendered your will and received the will of the Father? If not, why not?

_____

_____

_____

_____

_____

_____

_____

_____

Chapter 6

PUSH THROUGH THE UNKNOWN

"And we know that in all things God works
for the good of those who love him, who have
been called according to his purpose."
(Romans 8:28, NIV)

Have you ever wondered what your purpose in life is? You are not alone. Whenever I thought I knew what my purpose was, something happened to stop me from pursuing that purpose. Many distractions in life will get you off balance. The enemy can get to me when it comes to my finances. In the past, my finances stressed me out. If an emergency arose, I had to take care of it, which took resources away from me meeting my monthly obligations. I can remember getting so stressed that I would have tension headaches and tight knots in my shoulders. They would hurt like crazy.

Why stress about finances? We always say, "God will provide." We have to let Him provide. Where is our faith? Do we have to talk about what we believe in, or do we not believe? Other distractions are unforgiveness, hurt, and rejection. They take the focus away from God's purpose for you. Several times, I had to repent and ask God to forgive me for not trusting Him and having faith in Him. One minute, we are walking through life as if nothing is wrong. Then out of nowhere, a curve ball is thrown at us. It does not feel good at all. This is the tactic of the enemy to keep us bound in our thoughts. The enemy already knows our purpose. That is why he fights so hard to distract us.

We go through different seasons in our lives. Every season, our purpose may change. No, you will not know every step you must take right away. Open up your heart and mind to receive the download from God. A lot of the time, when we see the vision for our purpose, we run. We run from what it would take to fulfill our purpose, not knowing if we are qualified to fulfill it. My thoughts were, "I am not like them so I can't do it. I do not have enough training to fulfill the purpose. Why did you choose me to do this?" *Why not you?* God has a blueprint for each one of us, a plan for us to follow in life to fulfill His purpose for us. God's purpose for us is not just for us. It is for others as well. Humans can be so selfish. We always think it is about us. But it is about advancing the Kingdom of God and being an instrument in making it happen.

The distractions of life block the vision and purpose that were given to you. You become stuck and wonder, "What is my purpose in life?" You only see hurt, rejection, abandonment, unforgiveness, and financial binding. This is considered dead weight, anchoring you to the bottom and not allowing you to release yourself from bondage. I had to say a lot of affirmations to myself and speak life into my finances, my children, and myself. It was hard starting because my heart and mind were saying the opposite of the words coming out of my mouth. I remember that before I gave my life to Christ, the Holy Spirit was dealing with me. Yes, I had not received salvation, but I knew the Holy Spirit was pulling me. All I kept hearing was, "Come to me. Come as you are. Nothing you have done will keep me from accepting you."

I literally sat there and had a conversation out loud: "Why do you want me? I have done things that are not pleasing to you. I was pregnant at fifteen years and was made to have an abortion. From the age of fifteen years to that of twenty-seven years, I lived with guilt for getting rid of a life. How can you use me, God? I shortened my life. I do not deserve to receive salvation."

I am so glad He did not listen to me. When I finally surrendered and accepted Jesus as my Lord and Savior, the guilt left and never came back. So, you can see how distractions keep you away from God's purpose for your life. Surrender today and allow Jesus into your life. Each of us has a purpose. The Bible tells us to cast our cares on the Lord (Psalm 55:22). Once you do this, it will be time to go to work.

Achieving your purpose in life requires action. Not only do distractions cloud your vision and purpose, but you also take on sickness in the process. Your body becomes weak and you develop sicknesses like high blood pressure, aches and pain, and mental health challenges. God uses your body to move in His purpose for you. Distractions come and go. What matters is how you handle them and what you need to do to get back on track. Your family can be a distraction. When it comes to your family, especially your children, you will drop your plans to make sure you meet their needs. But you should not forget your purpose in life. God makes provisions for both. You have to stay in tune with God. Stay in alignment with Him.

Your first ministry is your family. This is why it is hard to recognize that your family can sometimes be a distraction. An example of this occurred when my marriage was being dissolved.

I realized that for years, I had met the needs of my family but neglected what God had called me to. Yes, I was saved, teaching Sunday School for the youth, leading a youth dance ministry at my prior church, and being a leader/teacher for TEN (The Eagles Network). But I was only operating on the surface. You cannot make full use of the gifts God has given you with only a quarter tank of gas.

When I realized what had happened, I felt horrible inside. First, I had disappointed God, and second, I had spent years sitting and not moving. I had wasted years not doing what I had been called to do. I had to repent to God and move forward. For the last three and a half years, I have been intentional. Distractions have continued to appear, but I have had to push through them. I have pushed through unforgiveness, fear, intimidation, comparison, and pride. I am not perfect, and I make mistakes and the wrong decisions even now, but I have learned over the years that I cannot continue to condemn myself. You know you have come a long way when you can recognize your distractions and shift your mindset from focusing on them. Yes, some of the distractions are hard to let go of. Let go, and allow the Holy Spirit to guide you through them so that you can continue to move forward in what God has called you to.

"Lord, I pray for those who compare themselves to others. We are made in Your image. Thank You for forming us individually based on the purpose You have for our lives. Thank You for the provision You have made for each one of us. I pray that we will realign ourselves with You and return our minds to You. Every day will be a new day for You going forward and not looking backward. Please remove every distraction from our lives so we can see the path before us. Remove the bondage of unforgiveness, low self-esteem, comparison, guilt, and loneliness from our lives. In Jesus' name, amen!"

REFLECTIONS:

1. Do you know what your purpose in life is? If so, what is it? If not, what do you feel it *might* be?

_____

_____

_____

2. What are some of the distractions holding you back from achieving God's purpose for you?

_____

_____

_____

_____

3. How were you able to get back on track from your distractions?

_____

_____

_____

_____

Chapter 7

FREEDOM THROUGH MY TESTIMONY

"And so you will bear testimony to me."
(Luke 21:13, NIV)

When you're going through difficult times, you keep your business secret. You do not want anyone to know what is going on with you. Do you remember that your parent(s) would tell you, "What happens behind closed doors, stay behind closed doors," when you were young? It has been three years since the Holy Spirit instructed me to tell my story. My reaction was "You want me to do what?" I wrestled with writing this book for three years. It is embarrassing to tell people what happened in my home. I have worried about what people will say or how they will react. Yes, I experienced infidelity in my marriage, but I am not the only one who has done so or will do so. A lot of the time, we go through things for others. We cannot help them if we have not gone through the same things.

Everyone has a testimony. This is my time to share my story. My story will help others to heal or get delivered. Being healed requires deep digging, not surface-level healing. The process gets ugly as you go deeper. I find myself whenever I have to face what is going on. I have to move forward even when it hurts. I refuse to allow my feelings to take over. At times, I feel like a robot—very detached from it all. Sometimes, I ask myself, "Why am I acting so nonchalantly? Anyone else would be bitter toward the world."

Believe it or not, I was bitter at first. The bitter me was not the best version of me. Putting a smile on my face may look fake, but it helps me. Those close to me indicate how important it is to tell your story. No one can tell your story for you. When I sit back and think of the different people I encounter daily, I am not alone. Many people just need encouragement and want to know how to make the pain go away. The question I ask God is "Why me?" The answer I receive is "Why not you?"

As the years went by, I shared a little of my story. Today, the hurt is not completely gone, but I can see that my life has changed due to my sharing and not holding back. Have I forgotten? No. I will never forget. The most important thing is to forgive, and to be the best version of myself. I deserve to be free. You deserve to be free. Besides forgiving others, the first thing I had to do to be free was to keep an open mind so that God could work on me. Second, I had to stay connected with the Father through His word or in prayer. Third, I had to obey what God told me or showed me. When you are free, restoration and deliverance follow. On some days, it was rough, but as you can see, I survived, and you will too.

During this process, I have gotten to know who I am all over again. As you transition from being single to being married to having children, you can forget who you are. You do not have to be married to forget who you are. Anything we put before ourselves for too long, without making sure we are not neglecting ourselves, will affect who we are as individuals. Personally, I was no longer my own person. Let me give you some examples. I'd be in the store, and someone would walk up: "Oh, I know you. You are married to...."

Another example is, "Aren't you the mom of...?" I did not think something so small could change my identity. When this situation happened, I had to take a long look at myself and ask, "Who are you?" I stood there and looked at myself in the mirror and asked, "Stephanie, who are you without your status, without your children, without your position at work or in ministry?" This was what I meant earlier when I said you had to have an open mind to allow God to work on you. I did not get to this place overnight, and I am still not at 100%, but I have come a long way.

Some years ago, my youngest daughter was having a conversation with my eldest daughter about me. My youngest said, "I don't know this Mommy."

Her sister said, "Oh, I know that Mommy. That is the real her, from before the marriage." I had to sit back and think about that. Had I changed that much over the years? When you become a spouse, you are no longer "you." You are "we." Your spouse and you become one. So I realized at that moment that I had lost myself in the process. You have to know who God says you are. I'm not just writing this book to tell my story; I'm also writing it so that others can see that they are not alone. I'm breaking off the additional chains that may be keeping others bound. As I write this book, I feel a burden being lifted. *Thank you, Father.*

You've tried to do things your way. Now, let go and let God do the rest. Love yourself enough to go deeper and see what is hidden inside you. Then permit God to raise you to the person He called you to be. Be authentic, and do not compare yourself to others. We all have unique paths to walk in life.

"Lord, I pray for those who have lost themselves in the process of dealing with the difficulties in their lives. I pray that they may open their hearts and minds to You to receive healing and deliverance. Thank You for loving them through their process. I pray that they may stay in their relationships with You to receive the plans You have for them. Give them the strength to tell their stories no matter how hard it may be. The testimonies are not only for them but also for those going through similar situations. In Jesus' name, amen."

REFLECTIONS:

1. What is the one thing you do not want others to know about you?

_____

_____

_____

_____

2. Have you shared your testimony with others? Why or why not?

_____

_____

_____

_____

3. How did you feel once you shared your testimony?

_____

_____

_____

_____

Chapter 8

Victory Laps

---

*"Do your best to present yourself to God as one
approved, a worker who does not need to be ashamed
and who correctly handles the word of truth."*
(2 Timothy 2:15, NIV)

While you are discovering your purpose in life, you have to do
some things to gain knowledge. God speaks all the time. We
need to be in the posture to receive what He is saying. Some
of us have tried everything but God. Try Him today. There are
blueprints for our lives. A blueprint is a plan set up for you to
follow. Everyone has one. We have to align ourselves with the
will of God to receive His plans for us. I can admit that there is
a plan, but I do not know if I am sufficiently equipped to follow
it. Over the years, I have invested in myself by developing new
skills or fine-tuning the skills and talents I already possess. I have
also developed spiritual gifts. Anything worth having is worth

investing in so that you may become a better version of yourself. I want to leave a legacy for my children and grandchildren. My mind is made up, renewed, and focused.

You are not meant to work on the plan alone. There will be others to help you along the way. With the resources and the gifts you have, you need to fulfill the plan given to you. When God gives you the plan, He has the means to get it done. Trust the process. I had to trust the process. For years, I knew God had called me to one office of the five-fold ministry. I heard Him, and He was crystal clear. You know what happened next: I ran. If you run for too long, you get tired. There comes a time when running is no longer an option. I had to surrender to the process. My response was no longer "No, I can't." It became "Ok, I will put one foot forward and watch you lead, Father."

Even if I had to go in fear, I stepped into my next. What is your next? He will not leave you on your own. Before the plan is put in full motion, you have to ask God to show you what is holding you back from achieving His purpose for you. I knew it would be painful to go deep into the reasons why I functioned as I did. A lot of the time, we suppress the relevant experiences and thoughts to protect ourselves from feeling hurt. God needs us to be willing vessels for Him during this season. The scars we have hidden so well are the distractions I mentioned in the previous chapters. They include unforgiveness, pride, insecurity, not being enough, and being unworthy. We should keep in mind that these distractions are not our identity. Jesus died so that we could live and have life more abundantly.

Are you living in abundance? What is stopping you? You will experience discouragement because the enemy does not want you to succeed. The enemy has already peeped at your future. Your development is not for you but for those to whom you are called. Those who are attached to you will benefit from the plan that was given to you. In my case, this is evident: All the courses and training I have taken over the years have shown my children that they have to work for anything worth having. There are no limitations other than the ones we put on ourselves.

"Trust in the Lord with all your heart and lean not on your own understanding; in all your ways submit to him, and he will make your paths straight."
(Proverbs 3:5–6, NIV)

Well, we are at the end of my story, but it is certainly not *the* end. We have journeyed from the early years of my life to how I found victory in everything God had for me. He wants all of us to reach that destination. Once I gave it all to God, the plan for my life was made clear.

You cannot go on this journey alone; you need a comforter. Trust in the Lord during the process of forgiving yourself and others. Don't stay stuck in unforgiveness. There are all sorts of distractions in life. Mine were myself, my family, and others as you have read. What distractions are keeping you from growing? My journey showed you that whatever we had done in life, God remembered it no more once we gave our lives over to Him. You should not pick up those past sins or old thoughts; leave them where they belong in the past. Your future is bright and full of opportunities.

You have to keep moving no matter how things look. Do not be satisfied with the place you are at. You have to forgive yourself and those who have hurt you. There is no room for pride in your life. You cannot live alone. You must die to yourself. When you are close to someone who is hurting, you want to be there for them. The same thing goes for those who want to be there for you. There is a blueprint for your life. Once you have given your life to Christ and stay connected to the source, God will reveal your purpose in life.

So stay aligned with Him to receive the download. It will not be a fast turnaround. Anything worth having is worth fighting for. Fight for your life, your children, and your purpose. Take time out for your mental health. It is important to make sure you are mentally healthy before you can help others. Life is short. Again, forgive the other person, pray for the other person, and see how your outlook on life changes. It is time to piece together the shattered fragments of your life. Taking this journey has revealed some deep roots that I had kept covered and had not wanted to expose. This journey to write my story has helped me forgive those who hurt me over the years. As well as everyone who is not out to hurt me intentionally. I am not all the way there yet, but I am striving to get there.

Hope, healing, forgiveness, deliverance, and restoration are around the corner. When unforgiveness turns into forgiveness, you will be able to see your victory laps in life. There is an award at the end of the laps. The award is a door that God has allowed to open. I am not where I want to be, but neither am I where I was over eight years ago. There are moments when I feel down, but when I think back and remember where I was years ago, I feel elated and grateful for how far God has brought me. Remember, you are not the only person struggling with unforgiveness. What story can you tell to help someone else?

"Lord, help us to keep our eyes on You. Your word says to study to show ourselves approved. I pray that we may be intentional regarding self-development and focus on You. We are to seek You and Your righteousness and all things will be added unto us. Thank You for Your guidance in everything we do. Father, please enlarge our territory in our region, territory, and nation. The harvest is plentiful Use us as Your willing vessels to increase the Kingdom. Father, thank You for taking us on this journey from unforgiveness to forgiveness, where we need to rest in You Instead of moving on our emotions. We come against the power of the enemy when we have havoc in our lives. He is trying to destroy the people You have called us to be. I pray for healing, deliverance, and restoration in our lives. These will bring forgiveness in our lives for those whom we keep enslaved. We know that once we align with You, the plans You have for us will come forward. Thank You for the blueprint You will release to each one of us. And may we be obedient to the callings in our lives. In Jesus' name, amen."

REFLECTIONS:

1. Do you know the blueprint of your life? What is it?

_____

_____

_____

_____

_____

_____

2. What steps have you taken?

_____

_____

_____

_____

_____

_____

_____

3. List the people you need to forgive.

_____

_____

_____

_____

_____

_____

_____

4. Have you taken the steps to forgive them? What were/will be your steps?

_____

_____

_____

_____

_____

_____

_____

_____

_____

5. Are you ready to tell your story to others? How will you do that?

_____

_____

_____

_____

_____

_____

_____

_____

_____

_____

_____

_____

_____

_____

_____

_____

_____

REFERENCES

[1] theconversation.com "Do people become more religious in times of crisis?" Trauma and Religiosity, Judith Herman, Mental Health Expert.

[2] lachristiancounseling.com "Learning How to Forgive: 8 Steps to True Forgiveness," 2023, Jessica Oberreuter.

[3] Merriam Webster, https://www.merriam-webster.com/dictionary/pride 2023. Pride.

[4] ACHI Magazine (www.achimagazine.com 2022).

www.ingramcontent.com/pod-product-compliance
Lightning Source LLC
LaVergne TN
LVHW021619080426
835510LV00019B/2650